FINISHING LINE PRESS

www.finishinglinepress.com

Where We Went Through

poems by

Nancy Nowak

Finishing Line Press
Georgetown, Kentucky

Where We Went Through

ACKNOWLEDGMENTS

Comstock Review: "Available Light"
Poeming Pigeon: "Seer"
The Bluebird Word: "After Hours"
The Paddock Review: "Where We Went Through"
Timberline Review: "Some Sense of It"
Willows Wept Review: "Beautiful, Until It Isn't;" "What Stays"

Publisher: Leah Huete de Maines
Editor: Christen Kincaid
Cover Art: Jon R. Leach
Author Photo: Jon R. Leach
Cover Design: Elizabeth Maines McCleavy

Order online: www.finishinglinepress.com
also available on amazon.com

Author inquiries and mail orders:
Finishing Line Press
PO Box 1626
Georgetown, Kentucky 40324
USA

Contents

For Jon, my life's Leach
(from Sonnet 50, Amoretti, Edmund Spenser)

"Grief has one great wish."
—Ellen Bryant Voigt

At Liberty

Dream what you will
if you can

don't dream
back what was

only pain—
return instead

to that tavern, listen
again for the girl's step

dance, her hard jig
shoes grounding her;

see despite
the cavernous dark

her brightness
and the round of men

from whose fiddle, pipes, bodhrán
a sound stream rises

while she has changed into light
slippers and, a doe

bounding through
a clearing, flashes past

all who watch, never turning
her glance as though

she might tell you she knows
nothing beyond this night.

Book Cellar

Down a clanging spiral staircase
to the basement catacombs, I am

drawn to the reason
in your voice
as you initiate a new recruit
into the mysteries
of arrival, dispatch, gain and loss

patiently bent to it, back
to the great dead tides
of authored shelves, to me

so at day's end, after we escape
to separate booths
in the nearby tenement saloon
dwarfed, darkened by an avenue of glass towers

I cross freely
one more threshold, press
you to seal a time for us to meet
here, soon, but one flight
above, at a rooftop table
alight, together.

Available Light

The need to see
drove us

one summer to Burchfield's
legacy, to Buffalo; the city lived in
lives in the artist's restraint.

His dry-brush watercolors, without rainbow
blue, banked lake, guileless sunshine
lavender-drenched petals

are iris-like
in how they renew
beyond ending. The painter

trusted his fugitive medium, tones
of earth, nimbus, ice
darkening as it thaws
would stay true in lowered light.

See in his streetscapes
a vanished city; clapboard houses weathered gray
are shades, too. He intended
the lidded windows, browed eaves
to look out at us

not like faces, our eyes
tricked by gestures of paint
but as though, still, his spirit
housed in them.

After Hours (Guggenheim Museum, 1984)

Day in and
up, elevated to the first
piece held in its cell, swarms

of visitors graze on
to the next, descending
away from
Picasso's late self-

portrait, his hungering gaze
you'd know, my love, if you could
close in.

No matter our rank, we workers
keep watch over
what at times feels ours, so

after the head guard
sends the last tourists spiraling
out and commandeers
the take from my Front Desk shift

like a bluff, beneficent
uncle, he sends me home

to collect you for a private viewing
proud to break an unwritten rule
no curator would consider.

The Museum glows, evening-lit
as you unlock
tiers of meaning in each

figure and gesture, each tribute
to forebears in a history
Picasso became
as he painted
his final night's work.

No one else ever
will know we were here
beyond the three of us
joined by the fourth.

Gamble

Who would dare
venture beyond the all aboard:

a Zephyr passenger
my sleeper's attendant offers, who
did not hear
her caution and vanished into
Reno, emerging in time
to hurl his coffee cup at the departing

train, like this one
that merely pauses, gasping for the next
breath, allowing me minutes
enough to pace the platform's length, return

when once
chancing escape, a brief
escapade at PJ's Lounge, we'd
cut across a grassy plot behind

the station where coach riders
queued for restrooms and glossy snack packs
alluring as the liquor bottles

cramming the bar's shelves, risk
only in a row of poker machines
stolid train attendants, vests
unbuttoned, played while we

ordered a Coors six-pack to go
back to our private window
settling in for
the planed landscape after Havre
and whatever else we'd
ride out, ever after.

Some Sense of It

I caught a scent, hint
of the sun's warmth
on the light air
turning like the path
toward spring

held onto now
only in words
retold while we take in
the burnt breath of
early autumn, Ponderosa pine
surrounding the High Desert

rest area. In a breezeway
display panels interpret
what lies ahead
with a map, what we might meet
in these woods

captured in nighttime
images: lucent eyes alert, bobcat and bear
sniff the air, grasp at the dark

 as we might try
to shape and keep what is
already changing.

Motif

Summer nights we'd listen
to crickets awake

in the dark, unseen
stridulent chorale, its

tiny repetitive motives
to lure, to court

we'd turn in bed
to words:

nearer, nearer, here you are
here you are, fearlessly, fearlessly

syllables we thought
we had corralled would modulate

change pitch and rhythm
quickening with the heat.

While You Dwell Within It

We call Sunday
our island, its borders

close as an embrace;
we nest within our
 quilt's fractal hem

until we want wider
hours, a greening
park's looped path
we move along

with other residents
of the same

language—once, a hound
trained in air scent rescue

baying, alert
as he sensed unseen
lives he might have led
to safety—

while the sky
drifts, pigeons swerve
into flight, geese

veer away
as though leaving

does not matter

then land again as we
return, tracing
this archipelago of days.

Shelter

The blue cedar's viridescent needles
feathered the branches
canopied over us while
in daylight we watched
a meteor graze the sky, spark, and

vanish. Bearing like the banished god
the name of mountains

our Atlas, its furrowed trunk steadfast
as a fluted pillar, could not
hold up heaven, even
time: we would not say
ever after, for

the wind could shift, sun
be hidden, unveiled
yet it seemed safe
there. The cedar withstood

one winter's long, soddening rain
until flood
turned blizzard. All night
snow-laden boughs sagged
then, defeated, cracked
and split, thudding against

the roof of the room where
we could not sleep
and were not harmed
but hurt

to see next morning
the broken, lost
limbs, how the tree
had been punished

like a god
laboring to sustain a perfect
sphere where all the stars
belonged, aligned, impossible
as Eden.

Beautiful, Until It Isn't

i. *Peter Iredale*

Morning's Scotch mist
harshens into downpour
palettes of Winsor blue and cadmium
sun will fix; *plein air*

easels clamoring for
the water's edge are painted
out, the shore unpeopled

the ship's captain, crew, two stowaways
brushed by this disaster all gone long ago
while mast, ribbed hull, remain;

the blessed wreckage—
may your bones bleach these sands—

now lies
composed on each canvas.

ii. Misawa

Torn from its harbor by tsunami
escaping, untracked, across
months, more

than a year, the dock—
the same weight and grief
of a stranded blue whale—
caught on this agate beach

is sea-stained, burdened
with ravening sea stars, kelp
that could smother a port

so it will be stripped clean
broken down, without time
to be rendered as landscape

although someone has painted a mural
on one concrete side, with waves
like stiff blue hills, brief memory
of a swelling, arched crest.

Ore Town

Over our orders of ale
brewed with these waters, specials
caught locally, we hear

a voice practiced
in delivering bad news
briskly, faceless

informing her booth
the river carries toxins
like a curse
to the mouth

where a ruined vessel
is now mired.
Once schooner, tender, tug
called back to harbor, its history
was meant to be
restored; instead its spruce keel
slewed, foundering
beyond recovery.

Spun from gold
slag, tailings, feed the current

unseen, she tells
what she was told:
shielded by a wing in Providence
the town's ill linger until

one by one
they slip away, lore she believes
accounts for the lostness
felt by this place.

Landscape, with Figures

Our own saint within
the Coast Range, a distinct ridge
not stripped of its fir

landmark rising each time
to greet us
travelers home

not by name, just as you and I
don't know

so call her after
Mont Sainte-Victoire, Cezanne's
beau motif, sketched
clouded, sunlit, drenched

then brought within
himself
to render again, once more
the true

landscape. After
we are home
the same rise, unmoving
reaches out to us

through a west-facing window
as though not in hours but a moment

just beyond that crest
we could reach, once more, the sea.

The Way Things Move

or, remaining, move us
as you and I
cross the Great Basin Desert

traveling by

West Wendover's towering Cowboy Will
who, neon winking, indicates East

a rocket garden, graveyard
of upright or toppled
missiles, a shuttle booster

and a monument to
the Last Spike, gold
driven into a laurel tie
marking where face to face
two engines, two
origins, once met

to stand above the Great Salt Lake.
At the strandline
Spiral Jetty appears
to meet us:

the Lake has shrunk back, revealing
a swirl of salt-crusted basalt and sand.

You find a way
down the sloped bank toward
your mission, walk its sole path, which
winds counterclockwise.

I watch, beyond hearing
as you journey
through the labyrinth
moving against time.

Where We Went Through

What
could have been
anyone's
undeterred easing
of breath; where

was our own
wrong, the place

on your chest
the cat sought
for warmth, or to pose
as sentinel, the way

we turned
from known bronze fields
after the winery steward's
generous pours of terroir

intending home, instead
driving deeper
into the shadowed valley.

Even though, as she filled
each globe, she warned
how an unflawed vintage
could be spoiled by
a fruit fly's signal
drowning, the ruin invisible

that winter would be so hard
we thought
it would hold long enough
for us to cross; instead

we broke
at an ice star, unsuspected
fault taking you
beneath a cold skin where
you still could be seen, I could
not see you through.

Fissuring

Those who left the well
uncapped, whoever nicked
the unmapped flowline
their undetected faults meant
a roar went red

when his welding spark met
air fused with a breath
of methane, not too
lean or rich, enough
to flame, burst apart
the man's home, and all

blame fell first
upon him, victim
who would never learn
how for years
scentless fugitive gas
had been seeping toward
the trap set for them both.

I heard something
like that shock, but
not that, words:

"I don't know why you're here":

the doctor spoke, looking down
at your file, life
in his hands

charging you with the failure
of some test—needle, image, probe—

As he made breath less
possible, I saw
your *soul or something*, a flash
of silk, escaping
out and out and out

not far enough, not yet
from that bloodless wounding
his first harm.

Betrayals

i.

Within the vestibule
of his ear, sound
became stone

the singing harp
of filaments
stolen away.

Before rain began
the air would shift
its weight, wavering
pressure stagger
him, numbed
to the ground.

Then when the dry season
worsened into drought, heartless
east winds
from the foothills
brought singed clouds
dimming the sun, the air
choked by drifted cinders, all

hinting how the earth
would turn
against him as
his sight
would be blurred, breath
stopped. Why

ii.

do I betray
a promise as I gape through panes
of a house no longer standing

as errant cells
felled him, as those who offered
no help or hope held a row of faces
up to his, ascending
scale of pain for him
to follow. Abandoned

iii.

across the scoured earth
an aftermath of leafing weeds.
Even the river thirsts.

Fire blazed
scree with a cipher
of runes, scythed
stands of pines.

The few gaunt branches left
once held green as
fiercely as fingers might
grasp a paintbrush. As he

iv.

and I once trusted
days of rain would restore
our place
steadily as breath
the swollen river continue
on its path. All the while

rising, it seeped
toward ground, an areal flood
overtaking garden, orchard.

Although it glistened like new morning
dank water hid smothering
waste. Receding, it left

v.

ruin unique
to each of us.

Saturnine

That god
is a myth, but
still we hope
the day called
after him

might give us
some breadth, an aerie
above the shore where

tented driftwood, rogue logs
uneasily settle, traces
of hidden breathing
pock the sand

while we perch
our wineglasses
on the balcony rail, brush
to the grass
a feast of crumbs

eager mouths
devour, unrelenting, all

we could want, this place as
removed from us

as his namesake
planet, its icy rings

no shield against
that lord of vineyard and plenty
who wields a scythe

narrowing time
until this day
we are
not spared.

Fatal Light

Outside another glass chamber
abandoned by morning
a wall stands helpless

sorrow, a stranger
who's been left alone, sinking
against its ungiving blankness.

While there is still breath, clamor
enters your ear's vessel
transforms through bone, pellicle, veil

into urgent voices:
it's all right to leave now
but where is it
you should *go?*

Until a new sound batters
your final sense, fledgling
sparrow brought to your window

by hard white
lamps never dimmed

visitant fallen now
from an illusive sky
to the courtyard below where

a downcast stone
angel waits, palms open so

if any voyage could be, you'd
stroke the still feathers, bent wings

all hurt lightly
angled toward release.

Speak of Leaving

The night my sister could say aloud
to her spouse *I forgive you*

eased absence; she felt her
sigh, settle
within her fired-clay spirit house.

But when I cry *I am
so sorry*, beg your forgiveness

I can be allowed
no answer
other than the wire
where a crow abruptly
isn't, or the hidden

garble of crickets
I drink in as your
murmured refrain:
it's all right, all right now, it's all right:

or the shelved volume, overburdening
the place it held, fallen
open to no loveworn image.

What Stays

The dark remains still
night sky dulled, no wonder

I dream you here

as the clouds fault
and light breaks through—
gloss of moon, glimpsed ladle, belt—
before shut off again;

across the river
a laded train
abrades the sawmill tracks
its chime horn warns
the unseen, unseeing
growing weaker.

Morning offers
a towering fir, red needles
burnt by thirst; a squirrel slips
down from bough
to bough, nearer
than you now

while a flicker's hammering claims
this territory
can be known as ours
no longer.

Widow

Who brushed against
me in the night, something more than
sleep wound
through my unrest, left

no mark, or one too fine
to see, too deep
beneath, a cap-
sized grief.

still warm
if touched, but
not hectic, no fevered
shivering after
that brief meeting.

Now in morning's
glancing light, a cobweb
of lines, like craquelure, that

evidence time
upon time
I smiled, pleased with being
myself with

you who might have seen
determined
in their design
how I'll face
staying on with you
gone, even though

little poisonhead
complicates the scheme
as she bears on her belly
a red hourglass, her
steady counsel.

Overwinter

Solstice, the sun
blamed for the hours'
least light while
the culprit
earth tips away. Ever after

the long unfavored
season appears
stalled in darkness
marking time

as anniversaries
of journeys taken
overtaken, ended
recur

we don't see change
though as branches relent
their burdens of snow
the days extend, reaching
toward equinox.

Seer

The cat backstrokes toward
sleep on my lap, his eyes half-lidded
after tracking hours of
February rain at the window.

The ear he tilts toward
the lashing storm
was notched by frostbite
wherever he lived before this shelter
otherwise traceless

as any past we can't breathe
back into being, precisely
retrieve. One Monday, some morning
a friend and I were not just eyes
above a mask, she told me when

she held her son and her daughter
in those scarce newborn hours
before they became *cute babies*, they'd

gazed at her, *curious, wise,* knowing
all answers they'd soon
forget, needing to join us
in searching for

a lifetime until
nearly leaving, any of us
might wake, once more
look that way, saying
It is very beautiful over there.

Nancy Nowak holds an MFA in Poetry from Sarah Lawrence College, where she studied with Thomas Lux, Jane Cooper, and Jean Valentine. While living in New York City, she also participated in workshops led by Louise Gluck and Joan Larkin. Her poetry has appeared in numerous journals, including *Poetry Northwest, The Sonora Review, Clackamas Literary Journal, The MacGuffin, the Timberline Review, Comstock Review, the Journal of Progressive Human Services,* and *Willows Wept Review,* and in the anthologies *The Zeppelin Reader, Windblown Sheets: Poems by Mothers and Daughters,* and *Last Call: The Anthology of Beer, Wine, and Spirits Poetry.* She has been a finalist for the *Southern Poetry Review* Guy Owens Poetry Prize, the Billee Murray Denny Poetry Contest, and the Letheon Prize.

She met Jon Leach, an abstract artist, in New York City, where they were married. She and Jon moved to Southern Oregon in 1994. After twenty-two years as an Associate Professor of Humanities at Umpqua Community College, teaching writing and poetry, she retired. Her beloved Jon died in 2020. She remains in their home on the South Umpqua River in Winston, Oregon.